# Softball

## Bernie Blackall

Special thanks to Michelle Frew, Head Softball Coach, Rollins College, for her assistance during the production of this book.

Heinemann Interactive Library
Des Plaines, Illinois

**Acknowledgements**

The publisher would like to thank the following for their kind assistance:
Rebel Sport, in Prahran
Students from: Armadale Primary School—Robert Klein, Nicola Murdock,
Khoa Nguyen, Mimosa Rizzo, Andrew Scott, Charlotte Sheck-Shaw, Zheng Yu;
Midway Elementary School—Whitney Tossie and Greg Tossie;
Keeth Elementary School—Alida Perez

© 1998 Reed Educational & Professional Publishing
Published by Heinemann Interactive Library,
an imprint of Reed Educational & Professional Publishing,
1350 East Touhy Avenue, Suite 240 West
Des Plaines, IL 60018

The author and publishers are grateful to the following for permission to reproduce
copyright photographs: page 6 John Iacono/Sports Illustrated; page 7 John Iacono/Sports Illustrated;
Australian Picture Library/Corbis Bettmann: American servicemen, page 8; Sport. The Library/Jacki Ames:
equipment, page 11

Designed by Karen Young
Edited by Angelique Campbell-Muir
Paged by Patricia Tsiatsias
Photography by Malcolm Cross
Illustrations by Vasja Koman
Production by Alexandra Tannock
Printed in Malaysia by Times Offset (M) Sdn. Bhd.

02 01 00 99 98
10 9 8 7 6 5 4 3 2 1

**Library of Congress Cataloging-in-Publication Data**

Blackall, Bernie, 1956-
    Softball / Bernie Blackall.
      p.   cm. -- (Top sport)
    Includes bibliographical references (p.) and index.
    Summary: Provides an introduction to the game of softball,
  covering the history, rules, equipment, and skills connected with
  this sport.
    ISBN 1-57572-634-3 (lib. bdg.)
    1. Softball--Juvenile literature.  [1. Softball.]  I. Title.
  II. Series: Blackall, Bernie, 1956-   Top sport.
  GV881.15.B53   1998
  796.357'8--dc21                97-31493
                                   CIP
                                   AC

Some words are shown in **bold,** like this.
You can find out what they mean by looking
in the glossary. The glossary also helps you say
difficult words.

# Contents

14.95

# About Softball

Softball is a bat and ball game played between two teams. Each team has nine players, or 10 if using a **designated hitter**, and a number of reserves.

The two opposing captains toss a coin to decide which team will bat first and which team will field.

The aim of the batting team is to hit the ball and to progress around the bases.

The aim of the fielding team is to retire the batters. They also try to limit the number of runs scored by the batting team.

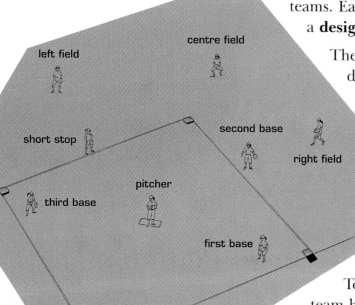

As well as the batter and the umpire, there are specific positions for the fielding team.

To score a **run** a player from the batting team hits the ball and progresses around all four bases. The batter must run from base to base, in order, without being **tagged** out or forced out. Being tagged is being touched with the ball when you are off the base. Being put out is when the base player catches the ball, and is in contact with the base, before you reach the base.

Each team takes alternate turns at batting and fielding. These turns are called **innings**. An inning lasts until the batting team is out. A batting team is out when three of its players are retired, or are given out. The outgoing batters then take their turn to field while their opponents bat.

The winning team is the one that scores the greatest number of runs after each team has played seven innings.

# U.S. highlights

Softball is arguably the most popular recreational sport in the United States with players numbering over 40 million. There are leagues and teams for every group imaginable including boys, girls, recreational clubs, and businesses.

## Softball in the Olympics

For the first time, in 1996, softball became a medal sport in the Olympic Games. Team USA was a favorite going in the competition as they had a ten-year record of 110 wins and no losses in international competition. Team USA earned the gold medal, competing with China in the finals, and winning with a score of 3 to 1.

The 1996 Womens Olympic softball team celebrates their gold medal.

# Lisa Fernandez— pitcher

Lisa Fernandez is one of the most well known softball players in the United States. As a pitcher for the 1996 women's Olympic softball team in Atlanta, she helped lead her team to victory and the gold medal.

During her high school career, she threw 69 shut-out games. While at UCLA, she was named All-American four times and was an NCAA (National College Athletic Association) Champion twice.

She currently plays for the California Commotion, a team in the Women's Majors, which is the highest level of competition in women's softball. She has been named ASA (American Softball Association) Most Valuable Player three times.

Lisa Fernandez

# History of Softball

Softball developed from the game of baseball. Softball was first played in Chicago in the 1880s. Players used a boxing glove for a ball and a broomstick for a bat, and played an indoor version of baseball.

The game grew popular and before long a new ball and bat were introduced. The ball was larger than a baseball, and the bat had a smaller head than a baseball bat.

Initially softball was played indoors in university and college gyms. But the game soon moved outdoors onto playing fields.

Softball grew rapidly during the First and Second World Wars. American servicemen played the game wherever they were stationed. They introduced softball to people all over the world.

At the 1996 Olympic Games in Atlanta softball became an official medal sport for the first time.

Softball, which developed from the game of baseball, was made popular throughout the world by American servicemen.

# What you need to play

## The playing field

Softball is played on a field called a **diamond**. Bases known as first, second, third, and home plate are placed on each corner. The most common playing surface is grass. The most common infield surface is clay, called a skinned infield.

The ball is pitched from the pitcher's rubber—which is directly in front of home plate and in line with second base. The **infield** is the area inside the diamond.

The **outfield** is the area beyond the bases and between the foul lines. The foul lines extend:

- from home plate to first base and into the outfield, and

- from home plate to third base and into the outfield

The batter aims to hit the ball into fair territory, the area of the field between the first and third baselines, all the way to the outfield fence and beyond. Anything outside this area is called foul territory.

When the ball is thrown and passes out of the playing area beyond the *dead ball lines,* play stops. Runners are awarded bases and the pitcher restarts play by pitching to the batter. When the ball is batted into foul territory, it is considered a foul ball. Runners return to the base they were previously on. No bases are awarded.

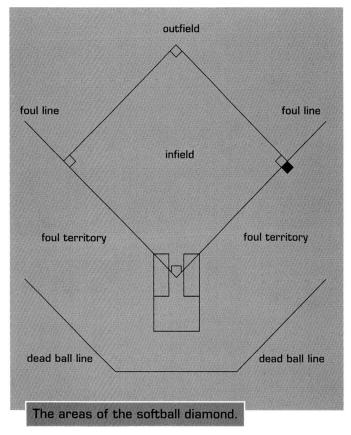

The areas of the softball diamond.

## The equipment

Most of the equipment will be supplied by your school or your club. Many softball players prefer to buy their own glove because it will hold its shape and fit their hand much better. Some players also buy their own bat.

# What you need to play

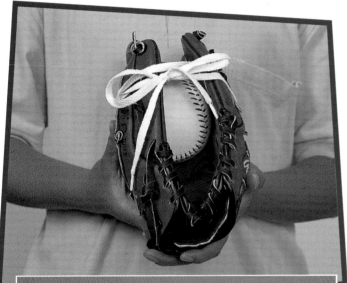

## Caring for your new glove

Take care of your glove and you will get the best wear from it. To create a good pocket for catching follow these steps:

**1** Rub some shaving cream into the palm area of your glove (where the ball sits when you hold it) and work it in.

**2** Place a softball in the palm area and tie the glove around it. This will form the pocket.

**3** Leave the glove for 24 hours.

Repeat this practice every second day until the glove has formed a good round pocket. To maintain this round pocket always keep a softball in the glove (and bind it up) when it's not in use.
Rub leather oil into your glove to keep it soft and pliable.
Never sit on your glove, flatten it out, or fold it up.

## The glove

While your team is fielding you will wear a glove on your non-throwing hand. Your glove should be comfortable and flexible—a leather glove is best. The glove is designed to protect your hand and fingers, and to make it easier for you to catch the ball.

The catcher and the first base player (the person from the fielding team standing near first base) are each allowed to wear a **mitt**, because they catch more balls more often. A mitt is a special glove with an enlarged pocket that makes catching the ball a little easier.

## The ball

The softball is made of rubber or leather on the outside and cork on the inside. Its circumference is between 11 $7/8$ and 12 $1/8$ inches and it weighs between 6 $1/4$ and 7 ounces.

## The bat

A small, light aluminum bat is ideal for a junior player—usually about 28 inches long and about 1 $1/2$ pounds in weight.

For safety, the batter, base-runners and catcher must each wear a helmet. Choose a comfortable approved model which which will also cover and protect your ears.

## The bases

The bases at first, second, and third are white, 15 inches long on each side, made from canvas filled with thick sponge not more than 5 inches thick, and are securely fastened to the ground.

In recreational softball, a double base is often used to mark first base. This base is 15 inches wide and 30 inches long, and is also made of canvas. It is fastened to the ground so that half of it is in fair territory and half is in foul territory. Half of it is white and other half is a color.

This double base is used for safety reasons. The batter runs from home plate to touch the colored part of first base which is in foul territory, and the fielder touches the white part of the base which is in fair territory. This reduces the chance of a collision at first base during close play.

Home plate is also white and fastened to the ground, but it is usually made from rubber. This is so that it can sit flat on the ground and runners can slide across the plate. The other bases sit higher so that when the runners slide onto them, they can maintain contact with the plate and not be out. There is no need for runners to maintain contact with home plate so they can slide across the flat rubber.

The pitcher's plate is usually made from rubber as well. The front edge is placed the required distance from the pointed edge of the home plate. This is 40 feet in youth and high school softball, and 45 feet in college softball.

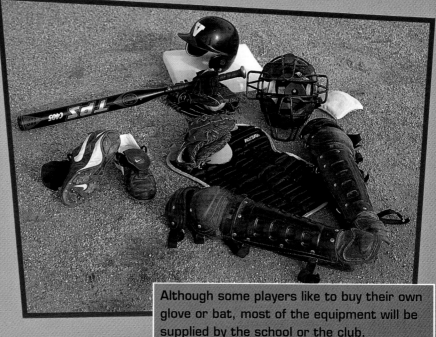

Although some players like to buy their own glove or bat, most of the equipment will be supplied by the school or the club.

## The uniform

The basic softball uniform consists of shorts style pants (baggy pants that stop just below the knee), a shirt in team colors and three-quarter length socks. Stirrup socks without a heel or toe are worn over the socks to help protect the shins and ankles. Leather softball sneakers with rubber **cleats** provide added grip when batting, base running, and fielding.

A helmet must be worn when batting, base-running, and catching. A cap is also good to keep the sun off your face and head.

As a beginner, whether at school or in a club team, you can wear your ordinary sports gear, such as shorts or sweatpants, T-shirt, and sneakers.

## Catcher's gear

The **catcher** plays in a difficult position. He or she stands close behind the batter to receive the pitches. The catcher wears a protective chest plate, as well as leg and ankle protectors. The helmet also has a face mask and a throat protector.

# Rules

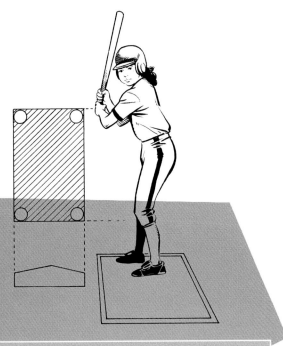

For the ball to be in the strike zone it must travel over home plate, above the batter's knees and below the batter's shoulders.

As in all sports, there is an official rule book that sets out the rules of softball. As you become more serious you may want to buy an official rule book.

## Pitching

The **pitcher** aims to throw strikes. A strike is a pitch that:

• passes through the **strike zone**, or
• does not pass through the strike zone, but is swung at and missed by the batter.

For the ball to be in the strike zone it must travel above home plate, and between the batter's knees and shoulders.

If the pitched ball passes outside the strike zone the umpire will call **"ball".** If the pitcher throws four "balls" the batter is allowed to progress to first base and can't be put out. This is called a **walk**.

If the batter hits the ball into foul territory the umpire will call "foul" and the ball is pitched again.

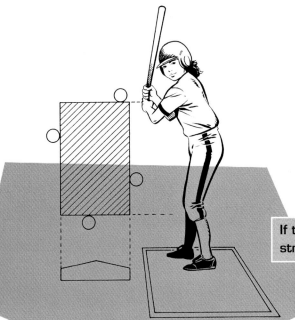

If the ball passes outside the strike zone it is called a 'ball'.

## Base-running

A batter who successfully reaches one of the bases is called a **base-runner**. Base-runners must remain on base until the ball leaves the pitcher's hand. Runners must run in a direct line from base to base. If they move more than 3 feet either side of the direct line to avoid being tagged, they are out.

## The fly ball rule

Do not leave your base when the batter hits a ball that can be caught. This is called a **fly ball**. If you do run and the ball is then caught you must run back to your base. If the ball is returned before you make it back to the base you are out. Only run on a fly ball once you've seen it won't be caught.

Stay on the base until the ball leaves the pitcher's hand.

Run hard once the ball leaves the pitcher's hand.

# Rules

## Tagging

Runners are out if they are tagged with the ball before they reach the base.

## Sliding

You are allowed to over-run first base, but if you over-run second or third you may be tagged out. (Over-running is running past the base rather than stopping on it. The runner must still touch on the plate to be safe.)

**Sliding** into a base allows you to reach the base fast, without fear of overrunning it. Sliding also helps you to avoid being tagged before reaching base.

Begin your slide two to three yards before the base. Gently fall onto your bent leg, lean back and slide onto the base.

## Forced play

On a **forced play** the base-runner is forced to run on to the next base because of an oncoming runner.

For example, when the batter hits a fair ball and there is already a runner on first base, the first-base-runner must proceed to second base so that the batter can run to first base. The runner is forced to run.

If the ball reaches second base before the runner does, then the runner is automatically out. The runner does not need to be tagged because it was a forced play.

## Double play

A **double play** occurs when two players from the batting team are put out in the one sequence of play. (A sequence of play is the play in progress after one pitch and before the next pitch.)

When sliding onto the base, keep your arms up so you do not injure your hands when you land.

foul

safe

strike

out

The umpire will hold up one finger for the first strike, two fingers for the second strike, and three fingers for the third strike.

## The umpire's signals

The umpire controls the play. As well as understanding the rules you should also be aware of the umpire's hand signals. There are hand signals for a strike, a foul, and when a runner is safe or out.

There is no hand signal for a ball. The umpire will call out **"ball"**, followed by the number of the ball—one, two, three, or four.

## Dismissing the batter

A **strike** is when a good pitch is thrown but the batter doesn't hit the ball or if the ball is thrown into the strike zone and the batter swings and misses the thrown ball. The batter is only allowed three strikes. After three strikes the batter is out.

Once the ball is hit into fair territory the batter must run to first base. If the ball is caught before it bounces, the batter is out. The catch can be in fair or foul territory.

The batter is also out when a ball hit into fair territory is fielded and reaches the base before the runner does.

# Skills

standard grip

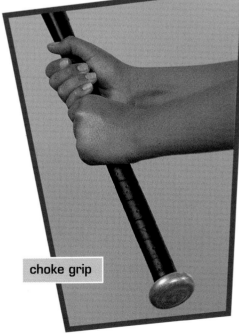

choke grip

It is important that every player learns the skills of batting and fielding. Each team will also need a few players who have special pitching and catching skills.

## Batting

The winning team is the team that scores the most runs. For the team to do this each player needs to be a competent batter.

### Grip

Choose a bat that is comfortable and light enough for you to control easily. Hold the bat with your lower hand just up from the base of the bat. This is the hand closest to the pitcher. The other hand should be touching against the lower hand also gripped around the bat handle. This is the **standard grip**.

A **choke grip** can make it easier to control a larger or a heavier bat. For a choke grip simply move your hands along the handle towards the tip of the bat.

### Stance

How and where you stand will affect how you hit the ball. Stand sideways to the pitcher. Extend your arm so that you are able to touch the furthest corner of the home plate with your outstretched bat. This is the correct position for you. The correct position will be different for each batter. It will depend on the batter's height and the length of the batter's arms, as well as the length of the bat.

Stand with your feet shoulder width apart, bend your knees slightly, and hold your bat at about shoulder height. Keep your head still. This is the ready position while waiting for the pitch. You should be relaxed and comfortable—and ready to swing at the ball.

## Swinging

A correct swinging action will increase your chances of striking the ball. Decide early if the ball is going to be in the strike zone. Once you have hit the ball, run hard to first base.

When waiting to receive a pitch your feet should be shoulder width apart and your knees slightly bent. Your weight should be balanced on the balls of your feet. Your front elbow should be at chest height and your bat back ready to hit the ball. This is the ready position for batting.

### Batting
Start with your weight on your back foot. Move your weight on to your front foot and keep your eyes fixed on the ball. As you make contact with the ball *snap* (quickly flick) your wrists as you hit the ball, then follow through.

# Skills

## Bunting

A **bunt** is a ball that is tapped slowly into the infield by the batter. Batters will usually stand in the standard ready position, then quickly change their grip and turn their body to face the pitcher. If the batter can do all of this as the pitcher pitches the ball, the bunt will surprise fielders. Bunting the ball often allows base-runners to gain bases.

With practice you will be able to bunt the ball in different directions. You need to turn your bat in the direction you want the ball to go.

This girl is preparing to bunt. When she's ready she will face the pitcher squarely with her weight on the balls of her feet. The fingers of her right hand will be hidden behind the bat.

# The position of the bat when hitting the ball

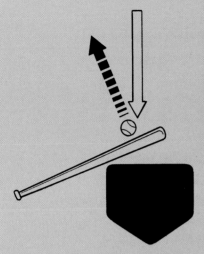

To hit the ball into leftfield.

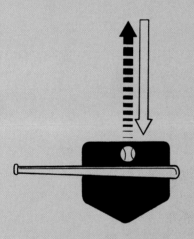

To hit the ball into centerfield.

To hit the ball into rightfield.

## Stealing bases

The rules of softball state that base-runners are not allowed to leave the base until the ball has left the pitcher's hand.

Sometimes base-runners will try to **steal** a base by running to the next base even though the batter doesn't hit the ball.

In school games the steal can often be successful. But in professional games, even though most runners can make it to the next base in 2.7 to 2.8 seconds, the fielders are so quick to react that the steal is nearly always out.

## Pitching

The pitcher is supposed to challenge the batter by pitching the ball into the strike zone. But a ball that passes through the center of the strike zone will be an easy target for the batter. When pitching, aim for the corners of the strike zone.

All pitches in softball must be underhand.

There are two main styles of pitching in softball—the more popular **windmill** and the less used **slingshot**. The arm action is the only difference between these styles. The pitching arm makes a complete circle in the windmill pitch. In the slingshot pitch the pitcher brings the pitching arm back and then directly towards the catcher.

# Skills

### Stance

Stand facing the batter with both feet touching the pitching plate. With your glove-side foot behind your other foot, hold the ball in both hands in front of your body. Step forward with your glove-side foot as you release the ball.

### Slingshot pitch

When delivered well, this pitch is accurate and fast. Aim for a smooth, continuous, coordinated movement and follow through strongly. Your arm should finish straight out in front of your body.

The ready position for pitching.

### Slingshot pitch

Stand facing the batter with both feet on the pitching plate. Your target is the catcher's glove—so watch it closely.

Start with your weight on your glove-side foot (your non-pitching side). Rock your weight onto your other foot as your pitching arm is extended all the way back and up.

Step forward with your glove-side foot. Rotate your body so your glove-side shoulder faces the batter.

Take the ball back, then down and through towards the batter. As you release the ball, push off your back foot and face the batter front-on. Follow through strongly with your throwing arm towards the batter.

The pitcher's grip for a low delivery.

The pitcher's grip for a high delivery.

## Grip

Grip the ball as you would for a throw, holding the ball in your fingers, not in the palm of your hand. The way you grip the ball will affect the height of the pitch. Place your fingers across the seams for a high delivery, and along the seams for a low delivery.

# Skills

## The windmill pitch

There is a greater risk of making an error with the windmill pitch than with other pitches, but when pitched well this is an exciting feature of the game. The ball approaches at high speed and it is a case of "batter versus pitcher". Practice it often. Concentrate more on speed than accuracy.

## Catching

The catcher must possess excellent catching, blocking, and throwing skills. The catcher must also be a quick thinker and a good leader. The catcher is the player who can best see the field, and so, is in the best position to instruct the team on particular plays. A good catcher is vital to the team.

## Stance

Stand about a bat swing behind the batter. If you are too close you could be hit by the bat. Spread your weight evenly on both feet. Your feet should be shoulder width apart. Squat down low and hold your glove open and facing the pitcher.

### Windmill pitch

From the standard pitching position rock your weight onto your front foot.

Raise the ball up and over moving your arm in a big circular motion. Step towards the batter with your glove-side foot.

## Receiving the pitch

Your glove is the pitcher's target so you must hold it very steady. Watch the ball leave the pitcher's hand and keep your glove open wide. If the ball is above your waist your fingers should point upwards as you catch the ball. If the ball is below your waist your fingers should point downwards.

As the ball enters your glove let your hand give a little to absorb some of the speed. (Your hand should move back two to five inches to cushion the ball as you catch it. This will help to prevent the ball bouncing out of the glove, and it will penetrate the pocket better.) Once the ball is in your glove be ready to throw the ball to a fielder if necessary.

The catcher in action.

Power the ball from your hand, releasing it at just the right moment to allow it to travel as fast as possible through the strike zone.

# Skills

## Fielding

It is vital that each player on the team is good at the basic fielding skills:

- fielding ground balls
- catching fly balls
- fielding backhand
- throwing

As the batter is preparing to hit you should be in the ready position for fielding:

- feet about shoulder width apart
- body balanced
- keep low, bend your knees, your weight on the balls of your feet
- head up, watch the batter

This will enable you to field quickly any ball hit near you whether it is in the air or along the ground.

## Ground balls

When the ball is travelling along the ground it is called a **ground ball**. To field a ground ball you need to bend low and catch the ball with your glove close to the ground.

## Fly balls

Fly balls are balls that travel through the air. You should aim to catch the ball before it bounces.

> ### Fielding a ground ball
> Move quickly to a position behind the ball. Lower your glove and bend your knees low.
>
> Allow the ball to enter your opened glove. Keep your throwing arm near your glove and cover the ball as it enters your glove.

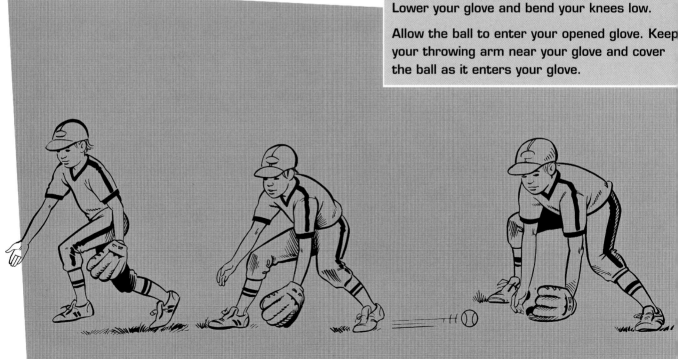

## Catching a fly ball

Move quickly to where you think the ball will land. Run sideways rather than backwards, and keep watching the ball.

Your hands should be above your head, your glove wide open and facing the ball. Your fingers should point skyward.

Watching the ball, catch the ball above your head over your throwing shoulder. Keep your thumbs together and give with the catch. As the ball enters your glove, cover it with your other hand, to stop it from bouncing out again, and prepare to throw.

# Skills

## Fielding backhand

Pivot on the foot closest to the ball and step across to the ball with your other foot.

Bend low with your glove elbow facing the on-coming ball.

## Throwing the ball

Hold the ball in your fingers – it shouldn't touch the palm of your hand. Your fingers should sit across the seams.

Move into a position so that you are side-on to your target. Keep your weight on your back foot.

Bring your throwing hand up past your ear, higher than your elbow, and back as far as it will comfortably go.

## Fielding backhand

Whenever the ball is hit to your non-glove side you will need to field backhand. Move across to the ball and stop it with your glove.

To catch a fly ball on the backhand side move across to where you think the ball will land. Your hands should be over your head rather than being low to the ground.

## Throwing

Whenever you are fielding you need to get the ball away quickly and accurately. Be aware of the play so you know where to throw the ball.

Players wear their glove on their non-throwing hand.

Move onto your front foot. Remember, a high elbow will make the throw more powerful.

Bring your throwing arm forward past your ear. Release the ball, moving forward as you follow through with your arm.

# Getting ready

It is important to stretch and warm up before exercising or playing a sport. Warming up will make you more flexible and loosen your muscles and joints. This helps to prevent injuries.

### Hamstring stretch
Sit on the floor with one leg stretched out straight in front of you and the other leg bent so that your foot touches the knee of your straight leg. Reach forward and touch your toes. Hold the stretch for 30 seconds. Repeat on the other side.

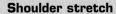

### Shoulder stretch
Hold your elbow and pull your arm across to your chest until you feel the stretch. Repeat on the other side.

### Calf stretch
Stand with your feet about a metre apart, one in front of the other. Lean forward so that your weight is on your front foot. Keep the heel of your back leg on the ground. Hold the stretch for 20 seconds. Repeat with the opposite leg.

## Neck stretch

Stand upright and place your hand on the other side of your head. Gently pull your head sideways until you feel the stretch. Repeat the same stretch on the other side.

## Thigh stretch

Bend one leg behind you and pull your foot up with your hand. You might need to hold onto another person or lean against a wall for balance. Hold the stretch for 20 seconds. Repeat on the other side.

## Arm stretch

Bend and lift your arm behind your head. Push the elbow back with the other hand until you feel the stretch. Repeat the stretch using your other arm.

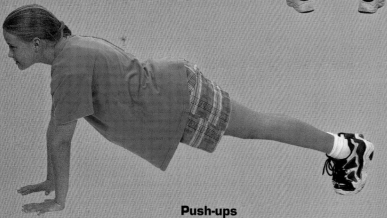

## Push-ups

Lie on the ground, face down, with your toes tucked under. The palms of your hands should be flat on the ground near to your shoulders. Push up using your arms. Keep your body straight. Lower your body down again. Repeat this 10 times.

## Squats

From a standing position bend your knees and squat down. Push up again into an upright standing position. Repeat this 10 times.

# Taking it further

Amateur Softball Association of America (ASA)
2801 NE 50th St.
Oklahoma City, OK  73111-7203
☎ (405) 424-5266

Cinderella Softball League (CSL)
PO Box 1411
Corning, NY  14830
☎ (607) 937-5469

National Softball Association
PO Box 23403
Lexington, KY  40523
☎ (606) 887-4114

## More Books to Read

Gutman, B. *Softball*. Tarrytown, NY, Marshall Cavendish, 1990

Jensen, J. Nitz, K.W. *Beginning Softball*. Minneapolis, MN, The Lerner Group, 1997

Walker, D. *Softball, A Step-By-Step Guide*. Mahwah, NJ, Troll Communications L.L.C., 1997

# Glossary

**ball** a ball pitched outside the strike zone that isn't swung at by the batter

**base-runner** a player from the batting team on a base or running between bases

**bunt** a ball tapped slowly into the infield

**catcher** the fielder standing behind the batter who aims to catch or stop any ball that passes the batter

**designated hitter** an extra player named in the batting order to bat in place of the pitcher or any other player each time it is the pitcher's turn to bat

**diamond** the marked square on the softball field with bases on each corner

**double play** when two players are dismissed on one batted ball. For example, the batter may be caught, and a base runner who leaves their base is also tagged

**foul** a ball that is hit outside of the playing area and into foul territory

**fly ball** any ball batted into the air

**forced play** when a base-runner is forced to run to the next base because the batter has hit a fair hit

**ground ball** any ball that hits the ground

**home run** the run made by a batter who makes it around all the bases and back to home plate in one play

**infield** the part of the field inside the diamond

**innings** a team's turn at batting which lasts until three batters are out

**mitt** a larger glove often worn by catchers and first base players

**outfield** the area outside the diamond but still within the foul lines

**pitcher** the player who delivers the ball to the batter

**run** the score made by the batting team each time a player safely reaches home plate

**slingshot** a type of pitch

**steal** when a base-runner runs from one base to the next without the batter hitting the ball

**strike** a pitch that isn't hit by the batter

**strike zone** the space above the home plate, between the batter's knees and shoulders

**tag** touching a base runner with the ball, or with a hand or glove which is holding the ball

**walk** when the batter is allowed to walk to first base because the pitcher was pitched four 'balls'

**windmill** a type of pitch

# Index